ABUNDANCE

POEMS

Courtney O'Banion Smith

Domino Dog Press

HOUSTON, TX

Domino Dog Press
www.dominodogpress.com
contact@dominodogpress.com

Book Layout ©2013 BookDesignTemplates.com

Ordering information and quantity sales:
Special discounts are available on quantity purchases by corporations, associations, and others. For details, please contact the publisher at the email address above with "Special Sales" in the subject line.

Abundance / Courtney O'Banion Smith —1st ed.
ISBN 978-0-9962311-2-1

To Nathan, Shepherd, and Asher for love

To Robert Lee Brewer for inspiration

To Sandy Dwyer for sanity

Contents

*To those who use well what they are given, even more will be given,
and they will have an abundance. But from those who do nothing,
even what little they have will be taken away.*

—*Matthew 25:29 (NLT)*

Preface

Let's begin by saying, before we begin, that the following is not all of what the poet wanted to say or exactly how she would have or should have said it; however, having said that, it's probably the best she could have done at the time. Therefore, following this bit about what's to follow, let's begin, but, before we do, the poet would like to offer a few words regarding her unending gratitude even if you

don't read another
word after these words about
the words you will read.

More of Less

We
used
to have
to wait hand
to pen to paper
like magic a message appeared
words meant something to the sender the recipient
an investment the cost of inconvenience and the effort
    made for precious time spent
now notifications' instant arrivals have killed
anticipation's aching and
communication's
artful cause
with less
for
more

Good for Nothing

prophecy if true is typically bad
in the short term at least
or it's not believed which is as good
as not being true and it usually isn't
but if it is and it is believed
it's no good most of all
for the prophet who says
I hate saying I told you so
but I love being right

Stranger than Science

Gravity
God's love
transcends
place and time
constantly attracts
ever closer
unchangeable
taken for granted
denied even
more puzzling
up close
one infinite
thing upon
which all
depends but cannot
be reconciled
on universal
or quantum
levels but
check the heart
that ancient
telescope calibrated
at creation
beats measured
in twos
a hole to
fall ever into

each to each
Him to you
come home
come home
come home

"The World Is Too Much with Us"

Would William Wordsworth still say that today?
Its defense was us. Poems and placards
weren't enough. New phrases like "tipping point,
climate change, environmentalism"—
greasy tools too slippery to work with.
Preachy to boot. We worked to break the world
we were given almost as soon as we
got it. But it's ours, by God, and we'll get what's
coming to us. Failed stewards, repentant
caregivers curate despair long enough
to use what's left. It adapts, never
needing us like we need it. We still do, though,
to know, to ever grow beyond what we
must see–this world's place in eternity.

Sevenling (Moon Between Earth)

After the lunar and solar eclipses in August of 2017

Moon between Earth and Sun,
darkness in daylight, celestial
awe reflected face to face.

Telescope pointed at the sky,
microscope at a drop of water–
stardust floats in every teardrop.

In the deep dark, all light shines backwards.

Power in the Blood

somehow something
gains access
direct contact
or breathed in
little white
soldiers go straight
to work
attack
no mercy
a remedy
a poison
in the blood
used to be let
leeches
sharp implements
just as likely
to kill now
let a fever be
to a point
body transformed
blood made stronger
through malady
if death's avoided
germs' gift
blood's remedy

Space City

Same as me, most people move here for work
or love's inexorable pull. Once here,
the gravity is inescapable.
An ugly sprawl accentuated by
tollways and impassable loops, this place
bulges over belts because expansion
is the mission. Infamous for traffic,
storms, and floods of Biblical proportions,
living here can be a crucible yet
a blessing; this place makes people, native
or alien, space or oil, neighborly.
Practical, we stick together. We choose
here for the loving grit and gracious gumption
that baptizes all who call home Houston.

You Are Here

A red star
an arrow
pointing where
a beginning
an A place
or another position
on the journey
path plotted
a trajectory
nothing stops
time's march
orients the pilgrim
ever forward
all moving
whether going
somewhere
or leaving
something else
headed toward
the same destination
an exit
map out
the black dot
not a full
flat stop
but an opening
right here.

As a Mother, I've Learned

there's only so much
of me to go around, yet
my heart grows, like the
universe, at a constant
rate. My patience–not so much.

13 Ways of Looking at an Apple

1

Dignified. Simple.
Classic lunchbox staple.

2

Shiny, mottled apples,
always waiting in a glass bowl,
mostly keep to themselves.

3

Cezanne's muse
and doctor's bane.

4

Every day at lunch,
sometimes breakfast and dinner
too, one crisp apple.

5

Not that it matters that she knew
better, my mother still tried
to grow an apple tree.

6

Never trust a snake
or a man, Eve said. Sometimes,
you can't tell the difference.

7

Bee and Sun's love child,
juice dripping down
my chin.

8

My husband doesn't care
for apples unless
they're baked in a pie.

9

Preferred breakfast beverage,
my boys probably consume
thousands of pounds a year.

10

Know which stores
have the best
at the best prices.

11

Conveyor belts must hate
them. Soft spots betray
careless cashiers and baggers.

12

Like coconut to summer,
fall means fake
apple everything.

13

Dignified until
you reach its core
like the rest of us.

Egg Day

School days mean cereal, but
if it's an egg day, he gives
his order: fluffy clouds with
cheese. Coming right up.

Disguises

Her boys—
armed, masked, or caped—
are themselves only when
she doesn't ask, "And who are you
today?"

Triangles

At three years old, a world of threes.
How old are you? He grins. I'm free!
Yes! (And no.) T-H's are tricky.

He knows—like brother, dad, and me—
he won't stay that way. Little boys
grow up (and out) eventually.

Triangles' points and sides of three—
crooked boat sail, your crayoned sea—
your favorite shape. Stay ever free.

Builder of Legos

He can't read
or remember what
Mama told
him to do, but he knows which
set each tiny piece belongs
to. Priorities.

Deconstruction

As Mom grows older,
our family grows closer
but still falls apart.

Daddy laid bricks but
built her a wooden house, now
dilapidated.

Elderly, Mother's
irresponsible, stubborn
as a mad toddler.

Who's responsible
for a life's wreckage after
old age sets up house?

An absence can grow
tolerable, but crazy
stays home, never leaves.

His ghost left, and she
filled the house to bursting–
a slow explosion.

They sought salvation
through salvaging things, so she's
made mass destruction.

Triolet

I never loved my body, and then I did
briefly. Transformed myself, but nothing stays
as it should. Constantly teased as a kid,
I never loved my body, and then I did.
Hated the scale, the pounds, the food I hid,
and exercise, but since suffering pays...
I never loved my body, and, then, I did.
Briefly transformed myself, but nothing stays.

Abundance

There is only so much poetry in
me, I used to think, so I dared not share.
Hoarding words created more scarcity.
My word problem was a matter of lack,
but faith's participatory, a trust
thing, ultimately an illogical
math problem of the two-fish-five-loaves-fed-
thousands variety. Besides, the best
chefs can work miracles with the simplest
ingredients, and words renew themselves.
No more fear, there will be no starvation
here. Just enough is as good as a feast.
Although a meager meal may be bread and fish,
simple fare, to the hungry, tastes delicious.

A New Day

always dawns but never lasts, so
you look back or forward
for better than the tired now:
an escape hatch or a bull's eye,
a fresh start you lose every time
you go looking for it.
Look.
       A beginning waits right here.
Better use it up until
every next time–
you only get so many.

Courtney O'Banion Smith lives in Houston, TX with her husband, two sons, and scruffy dog. A serious proponent of haiku and senryu, a dippy lover of God, and profound hater of keyboard courage and trolls, she will shamelessly defend the Oxford comma until her last breath. Despite periodic dry spells and distractions, she knows poetry still loves her as much as she will always love it. She is also the author of *The College User's Manual: What Professors Wish Students Knew Before the First Class.* Follow her on Twitter @cobanionsmith or visit www.cobanionsmith.com to learn more about her latest projects.

www.ingramcontent.com/pod-product-compliance
Lightning Source LLC
Chambersburg PA
CBHW021150020426
42331CB00005B/977